Nature Basics

Rock Basics

by Carol K. Lindeen

Consulting Editor: Gail Saunders-Smith, PhD

Consultant: Sandra Mather, PhD
Professor Emerita of ⬚⬚⬚
West Chester Uni⬚⬚⬚

Capstone press
Mankato, Minnesota

Pebble Books are published by Capstone Press,
151 Good Counsel Drive, P.O. Box 669, Mankato, Minnesota 56002.
www.capstonepress.com

1 2 3 4 5 6 12 11 10 09 08 07

Library of Congress Cataloging-in-Publication Data
Lindeen, Carol, 1976–
    Rock basics / by Carol K. Lindeen.
    p. cm.—(Pebble Books. Nature basics)
    Includes bibliographical references and index.
    ISBN-13: 978-1-4296-0004-0 (hardcover)
    ISBN-10: 1-4296-0004-7 (hardcover)
    1. Rocks—Juvenile literature. I. Title. II. Series.
QE432.2.L56 2008
552—dc22
                                   2006101953

Summary: Simple text and photographs present rocks.

Note to Parents and Teachers

The Nature Basics set supports national science standards related
to earth and life science. This book describes and illustrates rocks.
The images support early readers in understanding the text. The
repetition of words and phrases helps early readers learn new
words. This book also introduces early readers to subject-specific
vocabulary words, which are defined in the Glossary section. Early
readers may need assistance to read some words and to use the
Table of Contents, Glossary, Read More, Internet Sites, and Index
sections of the book.

Table of Contents

Rocks Everywhere

You can find rocks
all over the earth.
Rocks are made
of minerals.

Some rocks are
as big as cars.
Very big rocks
are called boulders.

Some rocks are
as small as peas.
Very small rocks
are called pebbles.

slate

Kinds of Rocks

Slate is a smooth
kind of rock.
Lava rocks are sometimes
rough and chunky.

12

Rocks can be many colors. Sandstone is red, brown, yellow, or white.

People Use Rocks

Many things are
made from rock.
Buildings can be
made of granite.

Polished marble is smooth.
People make statues
out of marble.

People walk on sidewalks
made of concrete.
Concrete has
many kinds of
crushed rock in it.

Studying Rocks

Rocks can teach us about the earth. Geologists study rocks to learn about earth's past.

Glossary

boulder—a very large rock

concrete—a mixture of cement, water, sand, and small rocks; concrete hardens as it dries.

geologist—a scientist who studies the earth's history by looking at rocks

lava—the hot, melted rock that flows from deep inside the earth and out of a volcano; lava rock forms when hot lava cools and hardens.

mineral—a solid in the ground made by nature that is not a plant or animal; minerals are found in rocks and soil.

pebble—a small rock

Read More

Cipriano, Jeri S. *Let's Look at Rocks.* Yellow Umbrella Books for Early Readers. Bloomington, Minn.: Yellow Umbrella Books, 2004.

Lilly, Melinda. *Rocks.* Rourke Discovery Library. Vero Beach, Fla.: Rourke, 2006.

Nelson, Robin. *Rocks.* First Step Nonfiction. Minneapolis: Lerner, 2005.

Internet Sites

FactHound offers a safe, fun way to find Internet sites related to this book. All of the sites on FactHound have been researched by our staff.

Here's how:

1. Visit *www.facthound.com*
2. Choose your grade level.
3. Type in this book ID **1429600047** for age-appropriate sites. You may also browse subjects by clicking on letters, or by clicking on pictures and words.
4. Click on the **Fetch It** button.

FactHound will fetch the best sites for you!

Index

Word Count: 118
Grade: 1
Early-Intervention Level: 17

Editorial Credits
Erika L. Shores, editor; Ted Williams, designer; Jo Miller, photo researcher

Photo Credits
Dreamstime/Areaphotography, 14; Brian Mcentire, 8; Cb34inc, 1; Linda Armstrong, 12
fotolia/Ivan Tucker, 16
iStockphoto, 18; Charles Taylor, 10; Mike Morley, 20
Shutterstock/Christopher Hall, cover; Dmitry Eliuseev, 4; Kanwarjit Singh Boparai,
    6; Victor Burnside, cover (three pebbles)